A Crabtree Branches Book

I0793931

Today's Stars

DRAKE

Ellen Rodger

Crabtree Publishing
crabtreebooks.com

School-to-Home Support for Caregivers and Teachers

This high-interest book is designed to motivate striving students with engaging topics while building fluency, vocabulary, and an interest in reading. Here are a few questions and activities to help the reader build upon his or her comprehension skills.

Before Reading:

- *What do I think this book is about?*
- *What do I know about this topic?*
- *What do I want to learn about this topic?*
- *Why am I reading this book?*

During Reading:

- *I wonder why...*
- *I'm curious to know...*
- *How is this like something I already know?*
- *What have I learned so far?*

After Reading:

- *What was the author trying to teach me?*
- *What are some details?*
- *How did the photographs and captions help me understand more?*
- *Read the book again and look for the vocabulary words.*
- *What questions do I still have?*

Extension Activities:

- *What was your favorite part of the book? Write a paragraph on it.*
- *Draw a picture of your favorite thing you learned from the book.*

TABLE OF CONTENTS

REDEFINING RAP

Most people have yet to launch a career by age 20. Drake was already well into his second career by then. At 15, he was a popular actor on a successful Canadian television show. By 20, he had launched his music career with the release of his first **mixtape**.

While other teens were doing homework in the evenings, Drake was writing and recording mixtapes.

Drake's energy, talent, and willingness to work hard brought him success. He helped support his family from an early age. Today, he often quietly shares his wealth by supporting people and charities.

While Drake first gained attention for his acting work, he has always had a passion for music.

Fun Facts

Drake played hockey but left the sport as a youth after a rough on-ice **cross-check** to his neck.

EARLY YEARS

Aubrey Drake Graham was born in Toronto, Ontario, Canada, on October 24, 1986. His parents divorced when he was five. Drake grew up in Toronto with his mother, Sandra (Sandi) Sher Graham. His father, Dennis Graham, lived in Memphis, Tennessee.

Drake mentions and promotes *his hometown of Toronto in his music.*

Drake's mother was a teacher who taught him the importance of education. His father is a musician who played drums for various bands.

Sandi Graham

Dennis Graham

As a child, Drake was teased at school because of his mixed race and Jewish religion. As an adult, he said he gets comments about not being Black enough. He just tries to be himself and not judge people's race or religion.

As a teenager, Drake attended Toronto's Forest Hill Collegiate Institute before transferring to Vaughan Road Academy. He later dropped out of high school.

Fun Facts

Drake is a dual **citizen** of Canada and the United States. He spent childhood summers in the United States with his American family.

ACTING UP

As a teen, Drake played the role of Jimmy Brooks, an up-and-coming basketball star in the television drama *Degrassi: The Next Generation*. His character was shot by a classmate and **paralyzed** from the waist down.

Degrassi: The Next Generation *aired from 2001 to 2015.*

Drake was a fan favorite on *Degrassi*. He played the role for eight years (2001–2009). He juggled acting, school, and his passion for music.

Drake left Degrassi: The Next Generation *after his character and several others were written out of the show to make room for new characters.*

The pressure of a busy acting career and a music career that started to take off forced Drake to make a choice. He quit school to focus on music.

Fun Facts

Drake studied with a tutor and completed his high school diploma when he was 25. He said graduating was one of the greatest feelings of his life!

SUPERSTAR STATUS

After releasing more mixtapes, Drake played in small clubs and went on tour with rapper Lil Wayne. His third mixtape gained a larger audience. Record companies now showed interest.

Lil Wayne was one of the top-selling hip-hop artists of the early 21st century.

Drake's first album, *Thank Me Later*, came out in 2010. It was a top seller, launching a **headlining** tour. He won Rap Recording of the Year and New Artist of the Year at the 2010 **Juno** Awards. **Grammy** nominations followed.

Drake has received 55 Grammy nominations over the course of his music career.

In the record industry, a platinum album equals 1 million sales. Drake has had many platinum and multiplatinum albums. Two of his albums have had six times platinum sales—or 6 million.

Fun Facts

Among his many awards, Drake has five Grammy Awards, seven Juno Awards, and 42 Billboard Music Awards. He has a record 13 number-one Billboard Hot 100 hits.

While his music career made him famous, Drake branched out into other businesses. He started his own record label, OVO Sound. It promotes young and new R&B, rap, pop, and soul artists.

OVO is short for October's Very Own, which is a reference to Drake's birthday month.

Drake also has a company that produces television shows, documentaries, and films. He has joined with other companies to produce footwear, clothing, and food.

Together with Nike, Drake has released his own collection of Air Jordans, called the "Air Jordan OVOs."

Many artists have the power to **influence** how people think and what they buy. Drake is that kind of artist.

Drake's fans are known as "Team Drizzy."

Drake's influence has been called "The Drake Effect." He has **endorsed** many businesses and their products. This has increased sales as fans buy products that have his support.

Drake has endorsed many popular brands, including Sprite and Burger King.

THE POWER OF DRAKE

The Drake Effect has impacted professional basketball. In 2013, Drake was made a global **ambassador** for his favorite sports team, the Toronto Raptors. He loves to attend games and promote the team.

As part of their partnership, Drake and the Toronto Raptors donated $1 million to fix up local community basketball courts.

Fun Facts

The Toronto Raptors renamed their practice arena the OVO Athletic Centre in 2019. The OVO owl logo hangs on the building.

Drake is known for his **feuds** with other rap artists. Some have been the result of competition and "sneak disses" in songs. Sneak disses are criticisms. Some are friendly competitions between popular artists.

Drake has had feuds with friends and musicians he has worked and toured with. Usually, the feuds are patched up. They almost always fuel album sales.

Drake became involved in an ongoing rap feud with rapper Kendrick Lamar in 2024.

Drake is a well-known artist who enjoys "giving back." He is known for donating millions to charities or small businesses. He also gives to people who are sick with cancer, need surgery, or need money to cover bills.

During a trip to Miami to shoot a music video, Drake gave out thousands of dollars to a high school, a women's shelter, and even shoppers at a grocery store.

Fun Facts

Unlike many famous people, Drake continues to live in Toronto, the city where he was born and grew up!

GLOSSARY

ambassador (am-BAS-uh-der): A person who is chosen to represent or promote a specified activity

citizen (SIT-uh-zuhn): A person who is a member of a country and has the rights and protection of that country

cross-check (kraws-chek): In hockey, the action of a player using the shaft of their hockey stick between two hands to forcefully hit an opponent

endorse (en-DAWRS): To publicly say that you like a product in exchange for money

feud (fyood): An angry argument between two people or groups that goes on for a long period of time

Grammy (GRAM-ee): An award given by the Recording Academy of the United States to recognize an outstanding achievement in music

headlining (HED-lahyn-ing): Appearing as the main performer at a concert

influence (IN-floo-uhns): To have an important effect on someone or something

Juno (JOO-noh): An award given by the Canadian Academy of Recording Arts and Sciences to recognize an outstanding achievement in Canadian music

mixtape (MIKS-teyp): A compilation, or group, of songs created by an artist, often a hip-hop artist

paralyzed (PAR-uh-lahyzd): Unable to move or feel certain parts of the body

promote (pruh-MOHT): To help or encourage something to do well

INDEX

WEBSITES TO VISIT

https://www.billboard.com/artist/drake

https://www.biography.com/musicians/drake

https://www.britannica.com/biography/Drake

ABOUT THE AUTHOR

Ellen Rodger won a bank-sponsored short story contest at age nine. It was the last thing her bank ever gave her for free, but it kicked-started a career in newspaper, magazine, and book publishing. Ellen has written hundreds of books for curious young people, on topics as varied as the history of the potato, urban wildlife, refugees, the Great Lakes, and explorers.

Crabtree Publishing

crabtreebooks.com 800-387-7650

Copyright © 2026 Crabtree Publishing

All rights reserved. No part of this publication may be reproduced, stored in a retrieval system or be transmitted in any form or by any means, electronic, mechanical, photocopying, recording, or otherwise, without the prior written permission of Crabtree Publishing.

Written by: Ellen Rodger
Designed by: Kathy Walsh
Series Development: James Earley
Editor: Melissa Boyce
Educational Consultant: Marie Lemke M.Ed.
Production manager: Candice Campbell

Hardcover: 978-1-0398-8030-6
Paperback: 978-1-0398-8390-1
Ebook (pdf): 978-1-0398-8150-1
Epub: 978-1-0398-8270-6

Printed in the U.S.A./CP2025

Published in Canada
Crabtree Publishing
616 Welland Ave.
St. Catharines, Ontario
L2M 5V6

Published in the United States
Crabtree Publishing
347 Fifth Ave
Suite 1402-145
New York, NY 10016

Library and Archives Canada Cataloguing in Publication
Available at Library and Archives Canada

Library of Congress Cataloging-in-Publication Data
Available at the Library of Congress

Photographs
Alamy: ZUMA Press Inc., p 6, Everett Collection Inc p 12
Newscom: Dennis Van Tine p 9 (top)
Shutterstock: John Steel, cover, title pg, p 14 s_bukley, TOC, p 17; Adam McCullough p 5, p 26, p 27; 4kclips, p 8; Kathy Hutchins, p 9 (bottom), p 19; Erika Cristina Manno, p 11 (bottom); Paul McKinnon, p 13; Ted Alexander Somerville, p 16; phil_berry, p 21; Wirestock Creators, p 22; Jonathan Weiss, p 23; Steve Cukrov, p 23
Wikimedia: Creative Commons, p 10, p 20, p 24
All other images from Shutterstock